Renée Forsyth and Jeanne Griffiths

A CHRISTMAS
A B C

with Illustrations by Annabel Playfair

SAINT ANDREW PRESS

For Joshua and in memory of Daniel

First published in 2000 by
SAINT ANDREW PRESS
BOARD of COMMUNICATION
CHURCH of SCOTLAND
121 George Street, Edinburgh EH2 4YN

ISBN 0 7152 0774 1

British Library Cataloguing in Publication Data
A catalogue record for this book
is available from the British Library.

Printed and bound by Bell and Bain Limited, Glasgow

A CHRISTMAS
ABC

A
is for
ANGEL

Far, far away, there is a land known as Palestine. It is in the Middle East. A long time ago in that land some shepherds were looking after their sheep in the fields. It was a dark night and they were watching out for any dangerous animals prowling about on the hillside that might attack the sheep. Suddenly a bright light was seen in the sky and an ANGEL of the Lord appeared to them. The ANGEL told the shepherds some good news – that a very special baby called Jesus – the Saviour of all mankind – had been born in the nearby town of Bethlehem that night. They would find the baby wrapped in swaddling clothes and lying in a manger.

B
is for
BETHLEHEM

The special baby's name was Jesus. The Emperor, Caesar Augustus, had ordered everyone to be counted, so Jesus' mother, Mary, and father, Joseph, as well as many of their friends, had to travel to the town of their fathers.

It was to the town of BETHLEHEM that Mary and Joseph travelled, and there the baby Jesus was born.

C

is for
CHRISTMAS

Jesus was also called CHRIST. This is from a Greek word which means 'The Messiah' or 'Anointed One' and that is why we call Jesus' birthday CHRISTMAS.

Although Jesus was born a very long time ago, He will always be remembered, and every year at CHRISTMAS people go to church and sing carols to celebrate His birthday.

D
is for
DONKEY

In olden days there were no cars or buses or trains, so Mary and Joseph had to walk all the way to Bethlehem. As Mary was expecting her baby she could not walk far without getting very tired. Joseph was worried about the journey and did not know how his wife would be able to manage. After a long search Joseph found a DONKEY for Mary and she rode on the animal all the way to the little town of Bethlehem.

E
is for
EAST

On the night Jesus was born the sky was full of twinkling stars. But there was one star which shone much brighter and more beautifully than all the rest. From the EAST there travelled three wise men. Their names were Caspar, Melchior and Balthasar. The wise men had studied the skies and seen this star and knew that it meant something special and important had happened – that a new King had come into the world. So they set out on their camels to find the King, and they found Him in the little town of Bethlehem.

F

is for
FRANKINCENSE

When the three wise men arrived in the town of Bethlehem, they saw the star shining brightly above the stable of an inn. They went into the stable and there was baby Jesus lying fast asleep in a manger. They didn't want to wake the baby, so they crept in as quietly as they could to worship the little boy, the new King, and to leave him some very special gifts. Caspar gave the baby a sweet perfume called FRANKINCENSE, Melchior offered him gold, and Balthasar left a special scented oil called Myrrh.

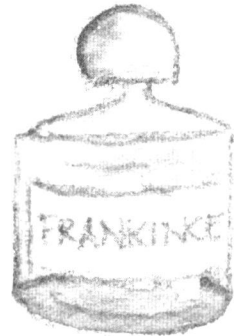

G
is for
GOD

Jesus had a father called GOD who lived in Heaven. Jesus also had a father on earth. He was called Joseph. GOD had sent His only son Jesus down to earth to save the world from wickedness. GOD wanted Jesus to tell everyone to be good and kind to each other.

Through Jesus, GOD wants to show people that He is everybody's Heavenly Father and loves all of us as much as He loves His son Jesus.

H
is for
HOLY

The three wise men knew that Jesus was the Son of God and a very special baby. They therefore called him HOLY. The word HOLY means pure in heart.

As Mary and Joseph were the parents of Jesus on earth they, too, were called HOLY. They are the HOLY family.

As baby Jesus was born in Palestine, it is often called the HOLY Land.

I

is for
INN

When Mary and Joseph arrived in Bethlehem the town was full of other travellers. They looked everywhere for a place to stay for the night, but there was no room at any of the INNS which were filled with people. However one INNKEEPER took pity on Mary and Joseph. It was nearly time for Mary's baby to be born, and he saw how very tired she was. He said to her, 'There is no room in my INN. If you like, you and your husband can spend the night in the stable, but you will have to share it with the animals.' Mary and Joseph had nowhere else to go, and that night baby Jesus was born.

J
is for
JOSEPH

JOSEPH, Jesus' father here on earth, was upset at Mary having to sleep in a stable when her baby was soon to be born.

But JOSEPH knew that this was the only place in Bethlehem that night which was warm and where she could lie down and be comfortable. So he decided that they would spend the night beside the animals.

JOSEPH worked as a carpenter and he dearly wished that he had brought his tools with him to make a cradle for the baby. Instead he laid the new-born boy in a manger, the place where the animals were fed.

K

is for
KING

Jesus was born at the time of KING Herod. Herod was not a good and wise KING, but wicked and cruel. Children sometimes called him KING Horrid!

Now Herod heard that three wise men had travelled from the East, searching for a new-born baby, a very special baby, who would become a KING. Herod was worried that this KING would be more powerful than himself, so he asked the wise men – Caspar, Melchior and Balthasar – to find the baby, so that he, too, could worship him. But the wise men knew that Herod wanted to kill baby Jesus, so they did not tell him that he was in the stable at Bethlehem.

L
is for
LOVE

Herod was a nasty sort of man. He did not LOVE the baby Jesus. But God, Mary and Joseph, the angels who told the shepherds the good news of Jesus' birth, the shepherds who left their flocks to greet the baby, the three wise men who brought their gifts to the boy, and all the animals in the stable – all of them LOVED Jesus very much indeed.

And as Jesus grew up, more and more people LOVED Him. At Christmas, when we celebrate Jesus' birthday, we give each other presents to show how much we, too, LOVE one another.

M
is for
MANGER

We have heard that there was nowhere in that cold, dirty stable for Mary to put her new-born baby.

When Joseph saw the animals eating hay in the MANGER, he gently pushed them aside. Joseph then filled the MANGER with fresh straw and made a comfortable bed for baby Jesus and carefully laid Him into it.

N
is for
NATIVITY

The day Jesus was born is called Christmas Day, but it is also called the NATIVITY. At Christmas-time, at school or Sunday school, children sometimes dress up as Mary and Joseph, with a doll as the baby Jesus. Other children dress up and act the parts of the shepherds, angels and the three wise men. This is called a NATIVITY play.

O
is for
OX

One of the animals in the stable at Bethlehem was an OX, which is another name for a bull or cow. In the time of Jesus there were no tractors or motors, so OXEN were used to pull ploughs and carts.

It was freezing in the stable on the night Jesus was born. The OX and the other animals wondered how best to keep the baby warm. So they huddled around the manger and their breath kept the little baby warm throughout the bitterly cold night.

P

is for PEACE

God sent His only son, Jesus, down to earth so that there would be PEACE in our world. The angels sang, 'Glory to God in the highest, and PEACE and goodwill to all people'.

Q

is for QUIET

Baby Jesus was born on a very still and QUIET night. There was an air of calm about, for the night baby Jesus was born was a very special one for the world. Christmas is a time to enjoy ourselves, but it is also a time to be QUIET and to think about the joyful birth of baby Jesus.

R
is for
ROMANS

Jesus was born at a time when Palestine was ruled by ROMAN Emperors.

There were ROMAN soldiers in every town and city and they made all the laws of the land.

Jewish people who lived in Palestine wanted to get rid of the ROMANS and they hoped that Jesus, whom they called the King of the Jews, would help them when He grew up.

S
is for
SWADDLING CLOTHES

Mary wrapped Jesus in SWADDLING CLOTHES when He was born. SWADDLING CLOTHES were narrow strips of material which prevented the baby from wriggling about too much in his crib. They also helped to keep the baby Jesus warm and snug while He slept, on that cold, frosty night in the stable.

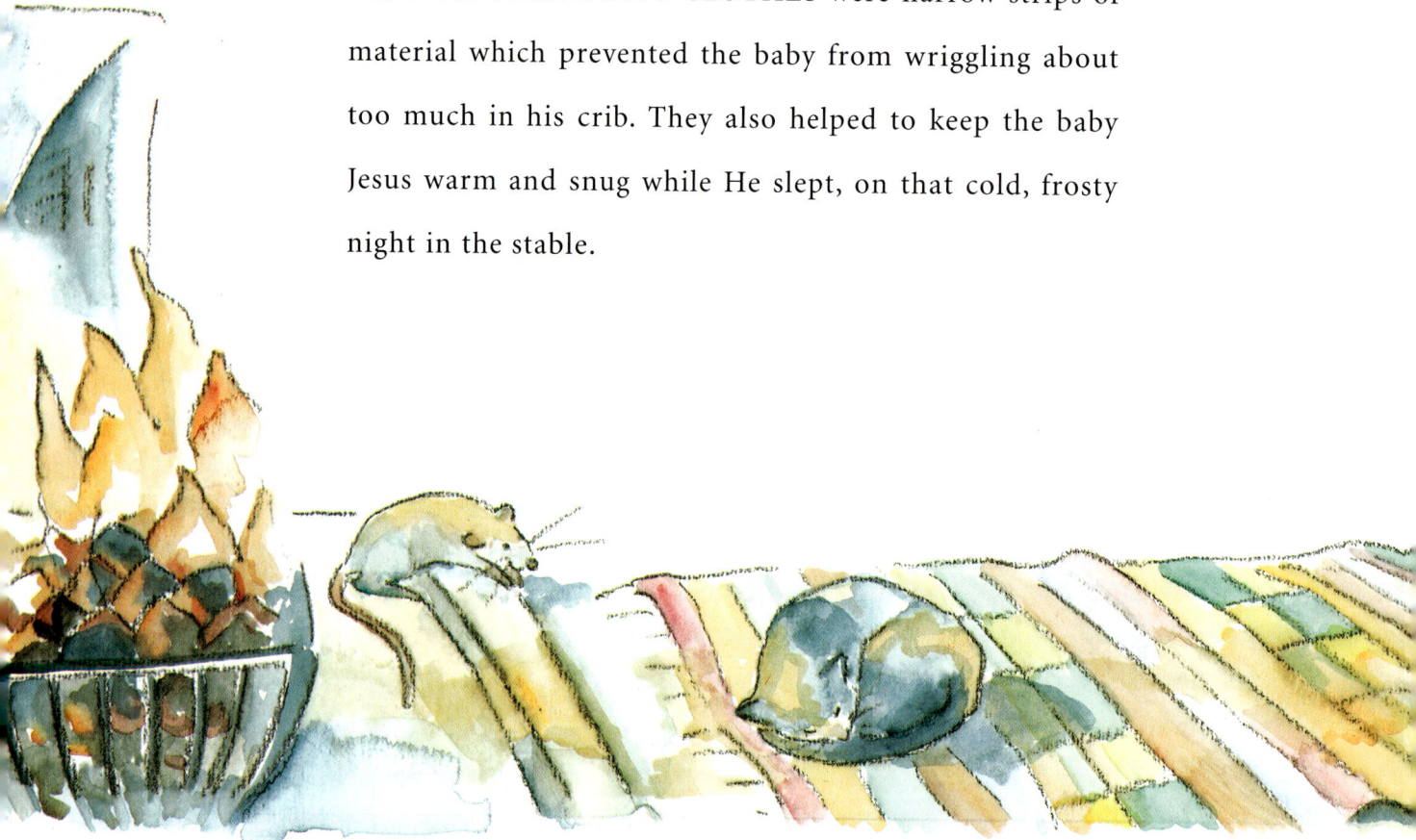

T

is for
TWO THOUSAND

Our calendar dates each year as 'A.D.' – *Anno Domini* – 'in the year of our Lord'. The year 2000 is therefore thought to be TWO THOUSAND years since Jesus was born. Although Jesus was born a very, very, long time ago, He will always be remembered.

U
is for
US

Jesus wanted all of US to love one another and not to quarrel or
to fight. Jesus wanted the lion to sleep peacefully next to the lamb,
and the wolf to lie gently beside the sheep. He hoped that there
would be no more wars and everyone would live in peace.

V

is for the
VIRGIN MARY

Long before Jesus was born, God sent a special angel, Gabriel, to tell Mary that she was to have a baby. Mary was puzzled by this. How could this be? She was not married, and in those days people frowned upon women who had babies before they were

wed. But God told her not to be afraid – she would have a baby who would be God's only son and He was to be named Jesus. Because of this, Mary is often called the VIRGIN MARY.

The angel told Mary that her cousin Elizabeth would also have a child. When Elizabeth's son, John, grew up, he became a preacher, telling people that a great King would come to them. That great King was Jesus Christ, the little boy who was born in that cold, draughty stable in the town of Bethlehem.

W
is for
WORSHIP

When we go to church on Christmas Day, and other days, we
WORSHIP God. We thank God for sending His only son Jesus
to earth to teach us to be good and kind.

As we have seen in this book, the shepherds, the three wise
men, even the animals in that draughty stable in Bethlehem, all
WORSHIPPED the baby Jesus. On Christmas Day, and every
day, we, too, can WORSHIP Him.

X

is for
XMAS

There are not many words that begin with 'X'. Sometimes people shorten the word 'Christmas' to 'XMAS'. But there is something missing from that word – it is 'Christ'.

When we are busy with the shopping and writing Christmas cards and wrapping presents and decorating the tree, we forget the reason we celebrate Christmas Day. It is the day that Jesus Christ was born – Jesus' birthday.

Y
is for
YULETIDE

YULETIDE is another word for the season of Christmas. The word comes from a time in the past when people celebrated Christmas by cutting down a tree and dragging a log into the house, where it was set alight to burn brightly.

Today, people sometimes make a cake for Christmas in the shape of a YULE log, decorated with chocolate icing and a sprig of holly.

Z

comes at the end
of the
ALPHABET

… but as we have seen,

the birth of Jesus is just the beginning.